A MESSAGE TO GARCIA and Thirteen Other Things

AS WRITTEN BY FRA ELBERTUS AND DONE INTO A BOOK BY THE ROYCROFTERS AT THEIR SHOP WHICH IS IN EAST AURORA NEW YORK, A. D. NINETEEN HUNDRED ONE

INDEX

GIFT

A MESSAGE
TO GARCIA

CREDO

I believe in the Motherhood of God.

I believe in the blessed Trinity of Father, Mother and Child.

I believe that God is here, and that we are as near Him now as we ever shall be. I do not believe He started this world a-going and went away and left it.

I believe in the sacredness of the human body, this transient dwelling place of a living soul, and so I deem it the duty of every man and every woman to keep his or her body beautiful through right thinking and right living.

I believe that the love of man for woman, and the love of woman for man, is holy; and that this love in all of its promptings is as much an emanation of the Divine Spirit, as man's love for God, or the most daring hazards of human mind.

I believe in salvation through economic, social and spiritual freedom.

I believe John Ruskin, William Morris, Henry Thoreau, Walt Whitman and Leo Tolstoy to be Prophets of God, and they should rank in mental reach and spiritual

i

insight with Elijah, Hosea, Ezekiel and Isaiah.

I believe we are now living in Eternity as much as we ever shall.

I believe that the best way to prepare for a Future Life is to be kind, live one day at a time, and do the work you can do the best, doing it as well as you can.

I believe there is no devil but fear.

I believe that no one can harm you but yourself.

I believe that we are all sons of God and it doth not yet appear what we shall be.

I believe in freedom—social, economic, domestic, political, mental, spiritual.

I believe in every man minding his own business.

I believe that men are inspired to-day as much as men ever were.

I believe in sunshine, fresh air, friendship, calm sleep, beautiful thoughts.

I believe in the paradox of success through failure.

I believe in the purifying process of sorrow, and I believe that death is a manifestation of Life.

I believe there is no better preparation for

a life to come than this: Do your work as well as you can, and be kind.
I believe the Universe is planned for good. I believe it is possible that I will make other creeds, and change this one, or add to it, from time to time, as new light may come to me.

I N all this Cuban business there is one man stands out on my memory like Mars at perihelion ❧ When war broke out between Spain & the United States, it was very necessary to communicate quickly with the leader of the Insurgents. Garcia was somewhere in the mountain fastnesses of Cuba—no one knew where. No mail nor telegraph message could reach him. The President must secure his co-operation, and quickly ❧ What to do !

Some one said to the President, " There is a fellow by the name of Rowan will find Garcia for you, if anybody can."

Rowan was sent for and given a letter to be delivered to Garcia.

How "the fellow by the name of Rowan " took the letter, sealed it up in an oil-skin pouch, strapped it over his heart, in four days landed by night off the coast of Cuba from an open boat, disappeared into the jungle, and in three weeks came out on the other side of the Island, having traversed a hostile country on foot, and delivered his letter to Garcia, are things I have

9

no special desire now to tell in detail. The
point I wish to make is this: McKinley
gave Rowan a letter to be delivered to
Garcia; Rowan took the letter and did not
ask "Where is he at?"

By the Eternal! there is a man whose
form should be cast in deathless bronze
and the statue placed in every college of
the land. It is not book-learning young
men need, nor instruction about this and
that, but a stiffening of the vertebræ which
will cause them to be loyal to a trust, to
act promptly, concentrate their energies:
do the thing—"Carry a message to Garcia." ❧ General Garcia is dead now, but
there are other Garcias.

No man who has endeavored to carry out
an enterprise where many hands were
needed but has been well-nigh appalled at
times by the imbecility of the average man
—the inability or unwillingness to concentrate on a thing and do it. Slip-shod assistance, foolish inattention, dowdy indifference, & half-hearted work seem the rule;
and no man succeeds, unless by hook or
crook, or threat, he forces or bribes other
men to assist him; or mayhap, God in his
goodness performs a miracle, and sends

him an Angel of Light for an assistant. You, reader, put this matter to a test : You are sitting now in your office—six clerks are within call. Summon any one and make this request : " Please look in the encyclopedia and make a brief memorandum for me concerning the life of Correggio."

Will the clerk quietly say, " Yes sir," and go do the task ?

On your life he will not. He will look at you out of a fishy eye and ask one or more of the following questions :

Who was he ?

Which encyclopedia ?

Where is the encyclopedia ?

Was I hired for that ?

Don't you mean Bismarck ?

What 's the matter with Charlie doing it ?

Is he dead ?

Is there any hurry ?

Shan't I bring you the book and let you look it up yourself ?

What do you want to know for ?

And I will lay you ten to one that after you have answered the questions, & explained how to find the information, and why you want it, the clerk will go off and get one

of the other clerks to help him try to find
Garcia — and then come back and tell you
there is no such man. Of course I may
lose my bet, but according to the Law of
Average I will not.

Now if you are wise you will not bother
to explain to your "assistant" that Correggio is indexed under the C's, not in the
K's, but you will smile sweetly and say,
"Never mind," and go look it up yourself.
❧ And this incapacity for independent ac-
tion, this moral stupidity, this infirmity of
the will, this unwillingness to cheerfully
catch hold and lift, are the things that put
pure Socialism so far into the future. If men
will not act for themselves, what will they
do when the benefit of their effort is for all?
A first-mate with knotted club seems necessary; and the dread of getting "the
bounce" Saturday night, holds many a
worker to his place. Advertise for a ste-
nographer, and nine out of ten who apply
can neither spell nor punctuate—and do
not think it necessary to.

Can such a one write a letter to Garcia?
"You see that book-keeper," said the fore-
man to me in a large factory.
"Yes, what about him?"

12

"Well, he.'s a fine accountant, but if I'd send him up town on an errand, he might accomplish the errand all right, and on the other hand, might stop at four saloons on the way, and when he got to Main Street, would forget what he had been sent for."
♣ Can such a man be entrusted to carry a message to Garcia?

We have recently been hearing much maudlin sympathy expressed for the "down-trodden denizen of the sweat-shop" & the "homeless wanderer search-ing for honest employment," and with it all often go many hard words for the men in power.

Nothing is said about the employer who grows old before his time in a vain at-tempt to get frowsy ne'er-do-wells to do intelligent work; and his long, patient striving with "help" that does nothing but loaf when his back is turned. In every store and factory there is a constant weed-ing-out process going on. The employer is constantly sending away "help" that have shown their incapacity to further the interests of the business, and others are being taken on. No matter how good times are, this sorting continues, only if times

are hard and work is scarce, the sorting
is done finer—but out and forever out the
incompetent and unworthy go. It is the
survival of the fittest. Self-interest prompts
every employer to keep the best—those
who can carry a message to Garcia.

I know one man of really brilliant parts
who has not the ability to manage a business of his own, and yet who is absolute-
ly worthless to any one else, because he
carries with him constantly the insane
suspicion that his employer is oppressing,
or intending to oppress him. He cannot
give orders; and he will not receive them.
Should a message be given him to take to
Garcia, he would probably at once refer to
you as a greedy, grasping Shylock, and tell
you to "Take it yourself!" He regards
all business men as rogues, and constantly
uses the term "commercial" as an epithet.
To-night this man walks the streets looking for work, the wind whistling through
his thread-bare coat. No one who knows
him dare employ him, for he is a regular
fire-brand of discontent. He is impervious
to reason, and the only thing that can impress him is the toe of a thick-soled No. 9
boot

Of course I know that one so morally de-
formed is no less to be pitied than a physical cripple: but in our pitying, let us drop
a tear, too, for the men who are striving
to carry on a great enterprise, whose working hours are not limited by the whistle,
and whose hair is fast turning white
through the struggle to hold in line dowdy
indifference, slip-shod imbecility, and the
heartless ingratitude, which, but for their
enterprise, would be both hungry and
homeless.

Have I put the matter too strongly? Possibly I have; but when all the world has
gone a-slumming I wish to speak a word
of sympathy for the man who succeeds—
the man who, against great odds, has
directed the efforts of others, and having
succeeded, finds there's nothing in it:
nothing but bare board and clothes. I have
carried a dinner pail and worked for day's
wages, and I have also been an employer
of labor, and I know there is something to
be said on both sides. There is no excellence, per se, in poverty; rags are no recommendation; and all employers are not
rapacious and high handed, any more than
all poor men are virtuous. My heart goes

15

A MESSAGE
TO GARCIA
out to the man who does his work when the "boss" is away, as well as when he is at home. And the man, who, when given a letter for Garcia, quietly takes the missive, without asking any idiotic questions, and with no lurking intention of chucking it into the nearest sewer, or of doing aught else but deliver it, never gets "laid off," nor has to go on a strike for higher wages. Civilization is one long anxious search for just such individuals. Anything such a man asks shall be granted. He is wanted in every city, town and village—in every office, shop, store and factory. The world cries out for such: he is needed, and is needed badly—the man who can carry a message to Garcia.

THE EX-LIBRIS COLLECTOR

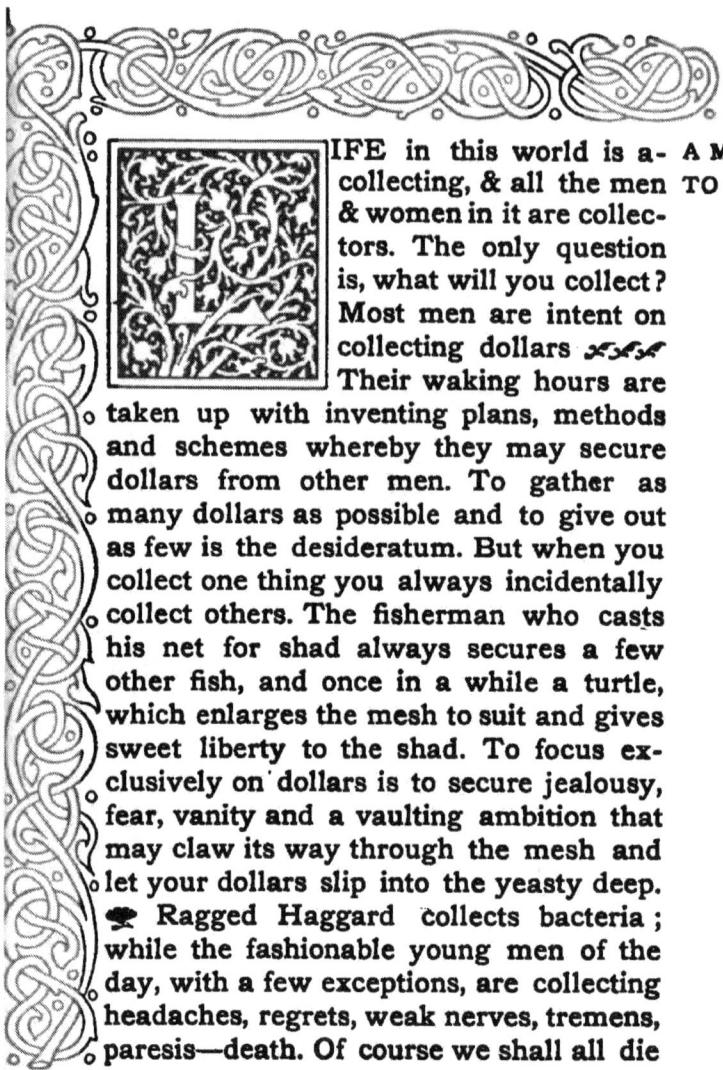

LIFE in this world is a-collecting, & all the men & women in it are collectors. The only question is, what will you collect? Most men are intent on collecting dollars ✘✘✘✘ Their waking hours are taken up with inventing plans, methods and schemes whereby they may secure dollars from other men. To gather as many dollars as possible and to give out as few is the desideratum. But when you collect one thing you always incidentally collect others. The fisherman who casts his net for shad always secures a few other fish, and once in a while a turtle, which enlarges the mesh to suit and gives sweet liberty to the shad. To focus exclusively on dollars is to secure jealousy, fear, vanity and a vaulting ambition that may claw its way through the mesh and let your dollars slip into the yeasty deep. ♣ Ragged Haggard collects bacteria; while the fashionable young men of the day, with a few exceptions, are collecting headaches, regrets, weak nerves, tremens, paresis—death. Of course we shall all die

21

(I 'll admit that), and further, we may be a
long time dead (I 'll admit that), and further, we may be going through the world
for the last time—as to that I do not know
—but while we are here it seems the part
of reason to devote our energies to that
which brings as few heart-pangs to ourselves and others as possible. We are here,
and some day we must go, and surely we
would like to depart gracefully.

Now, I do not know exactly why men collect book-plates. But I think I have traced
out a very little of the psychology of collecting. And first I would call your attention to the fact that no one ever went off,
secretly and by stealth, and collected
book-plates, as a miser hoards and gloats
over his gold.

The collector's cast of mind is totally different from that of the miser. The miser
loves the gold for its own sake—the collector loves a book-plate for what it sug-
gests. In other words, he does not love a
book-plate at all. He may think he does,
but he does n't; he holds it in solution and
when the time is ripe he sheds it as a
snake sheds its skin; whereas the miser
hoards till he dies, and dying, clutches 🐝

22

Witness, if you please, Mr. James Fraser
Gluck collecting autographs and such tri-
fles industriously and intensely for years,
paying out thousands of dollars and then
one fine day presenting the whole collection to the Buffalo Library. And this while
he was a young man.
Dozens of such cases could be cited to
prove that the mania sits lightly, and like
the whole material world is of small account to the man who can get off at a
distance and take a good look at it.
No collector ever evolved the craze alone;
he is exposed and catches it. Where you
see one man collecting, around the corner
you 'll find another. The psychic basis of
collecting is human sympathy, and not a
mere lust for possession ✈ You collect
because someone you admire collects,
although I do not ask you to confess this
before men. You exchange plates and at
the same time you exchange courtesy,
kindliness and mutual good will. Having
the book-plate of a collector you are
pledged to that man by a tie which is very
gentle, yet very strong. He does not dictate to you, nor rob you of your time, nor
intrude his personality upon you, but from

out of the unseen now and again comes a
cheery message (and a book-plate) and
you send back good cheer and kindly
greetings (and a book-plate, for some one
has sent you duplicates).

And thus the circle grows until all 'round
the world you count your friends and
brothers, held together by the mystic
bond, which binds men who love the same
things and are engaged in like pursuits.
Then beyond this you are linked to the
past by the plates you own of men now
dust, and you know, too, all the men who
have wrought & traced in lines of beauty,
and thought and felt and suffered and en-
joyed. You know them all—you know
their successes and defeats, their hopes
and sorrows.

You do not say that Holbein and Hogarth
were, you say they are, for you have their
work—they are immortal. And so you
confuse the dead and living in one fairy
company, and although you detect vary-
ing degrees of excellence, for none do you
hold contempt, of none are you jealous—
none do you envy.

From them you ask nothing, upon you
they make no demands, save that their

friendship shall be frank, free, unselfish &
unsullied 🐚

It is not at all necessary to meet a collector face to face in order to hold sweet converse. By their plates ye shall know them. And so I have avoided meeting my dear friends, more than once, that the delicacy of the relationship should not be disturbed. But sometimes I break the rule, and being in New Haven not long ago I called on Mr. W. F. Hopson. In the yard back of his house Hopson has a pretty little studio, made of matched pine, and the whole thing must have cost him fifty dollars. The light comes in from the roof, as it does in the Church of the Madeleine and the Chapel of Pere la Chaise, save for a beautiful north window which was evidently pinched by Hopson from some Italian chapel, although he swears differently 🖙

Together we called on Mr. George Dudley Seymour and Mr. Everett E. Lord. Seymour has posters and china and bookplates and brocades, all representing the beautiful handiwork of men long dead. Lord has a collection of prints which cost him ten thousand dollars, gathered over

25

the space of twenty years. But the point I wish to make is that as the treasures were brought forth and shown, the comments revealed the names of Woodbury, Bolles, Allen, Dodge, Shir-Cliff, Woodworth, Ellsworth, Gobeille, Humphreys, Mack, French, Rhead, and all those other choice spirits, who are my friends, and whose presence in my thoughts takes the bitterness out of life and gives a solace when all my hopes seem gone. The friends of these men are my friends, too; so we were as brothers.

Then the next day I went up to Hartford and saw Mr. Charles Dexter Allen, who has an absurd head of hair and many book-plates; and then on to Boston where I called on Mr. John P. Woodbury, who has a long white beard and a grace and dignity which make you think of Michael Angelo's Moses. Mr. Woodbury has a great collection of French's book-plates, and others galore, the most valuable collection of "The Compleat Angler" in the world, and extra-illustrated books & first editions until 't would make you dizzy to tell you of them. And whom did we talk about as we looked at the treasures? I 'll

26

tell you—we talked of Bolles, Stone, Shir-
Cliff, Dering, Allen, Dodge, Woodworth,
Ellsworth, Gobeille, Rhead, Humphreys,
French, and all those other friends who
are both his and mine. Mr. Woodbury is
nearly the Ideal Collector :—he has lived
his three score and ten, but his eye is as
bright as a boy's, his complexion as fair as
a baby's, and he carries with him the per-
fume of the morning and the lavish heart
of youth ❧
And so a fad which gives joy without
headache, peace without stupor, & friends
who are not rivals, is worth cultivating;
at least I think so. Its basis is human sympathy, & its excuse for being—book-plates.

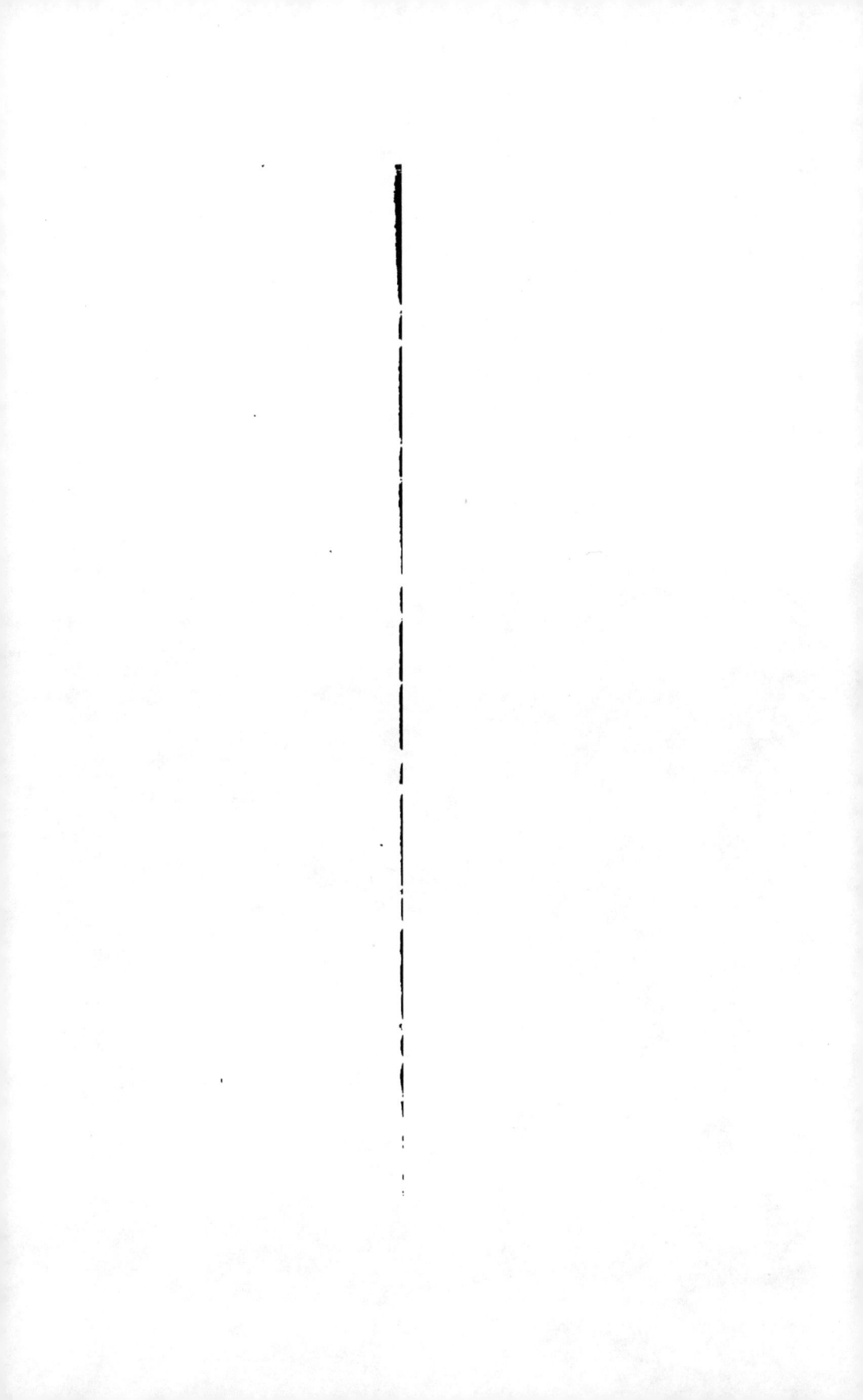

THE SOCIAL
EXODUS

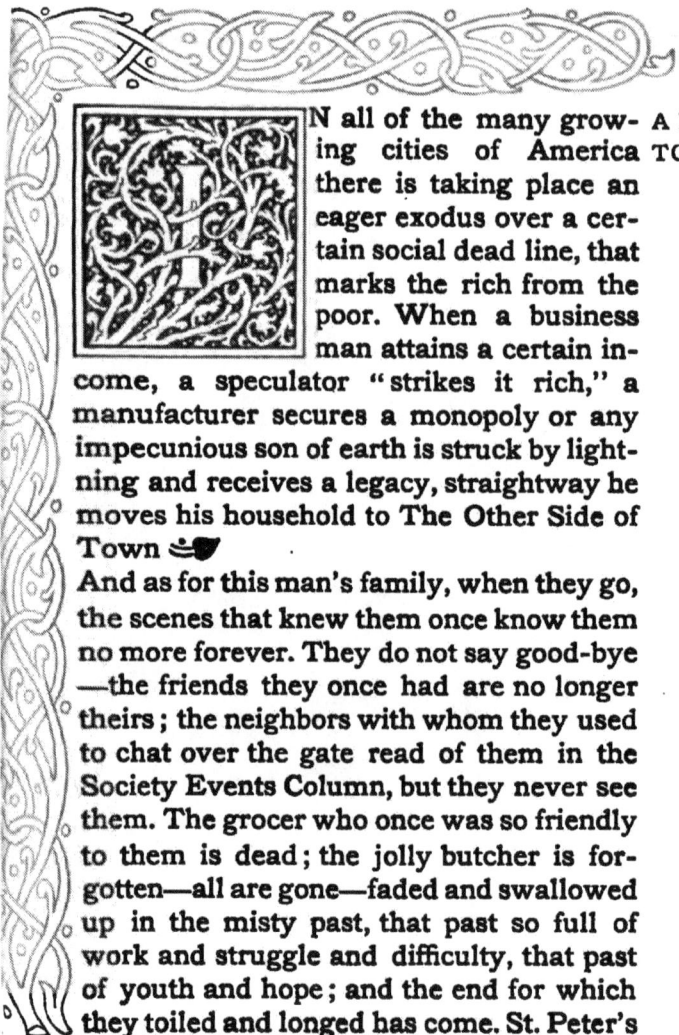

I N all of the many growing cities of America there is taking place an eager exodus over a certain social dead line, that marks the rich from the poor. When a business man attains a certain income, a speculator "strikes it rich," a manufacturer secures a monopoly or any impecunious son of earth is struck by lightning and receives a legacy, straightway he moves his household to The Other Side of Town ☙

And as for this man's family, when they go, the scenes that knew them once know them no more forever. They do not say good-bye —the friends they once had are no longer theirs; the neighbors with whom they used to chat over the gate read of them in the Society Events Column, but they never see them. The grocer who once was so friendly to them is dead; the jolly butcher is forgotten—all are gone—faded and swallowed up in the misty past, that past so full of work and struggle and difficulty, that past of youth and hope; and the end for which they toiled and longed has come. St. Peter's

33

golden gates have opened: they have
moved to the Other Side.

Men who have incomes of four thousand
dollars or more, in Buffalo, make hot haste
to live on Delaware Avenue; in Pittsburg
it is the East End; in Cincinnati, Walnut
Hills; in Cleveland, Euclid Avenue; in
Chicago, Hyde Park; in Boston, Commonwealth Avenue; in New York, Up-Town.
❧ And in these social migrations there is
something pitiful, wondrous pitiful; for the
man who goes can never return of his own
free will; and to be forced back by fate is
to suffer a humiliation that is worse than
disgrace that comes through crime. When
a rich man, say in Albany, Syracuse or
Toledo, loses his money and his family has
to " come down," the sympathetic souls of
earth shed tears for the glory that is gone.
We tell how he has had to give up all—he
gave up his horses, his billiard tables, his
solid plate: he discharged his gardener, his
coachman, his butler. He is now keeping
books for twenty dollars a week and his
wife is doing her own work: and we relate
how his children are now compelled to
attend the public school ❧ Ah, me! Life is
grievous, and our days are full of trouble!

34

On questioning a good many men who have taken part in the Social Exodus, I find that, Adam-like, the responsibility of the change is thrown entirely on the woman: " My wife was dissatisfied and we had to go." Not once could I ever get a man to acknowledge that the question of pride, the desire to parade his success, or the hope of a better social position for his daughters ever weighed in the scale. But then a man is seldom aware of the motives that move him : we deceive ourselves and hide behind specious pleas of many hues.

The women of the Exodus tell me that the reason they moved to Commonwealth Avenue was because the sewerage was imperfect in the old home, the water was bad, the air full of smoke, or the neighbors' children rude And in various instances these worthy mothers following the example of their husbands, unloaded the responsibility on the children. " When Mayme came home from Wellesley she could not stand it here," or " When George got back from Harvard he found the society so awfully dull."

And right here let us note this prevalent fact: the first effect of College life is often

35

a desire to separate from the old companions—a drawing away from the plain and
simple; a separation from the mass and a
making of cliques; an unfitting for life's
commonplace duties and the forming of a
condition that makes riches a necessity
and their loss a calamity.

That much of our so-called "culture" has
been bought at the price of manhood, no
one who knows men can deny. But when
matters go far enough in any one direction
the pendulum swings back and they cure
themselves: and now behold the College
Settlement! That the men and women of
wealth and culture who are deliberately
making their homes among the poor are as
one to ten thousand, compared with the
"sudden rich" who are making frantic
efforts to get away from all smirching contact with plain people, there is no doubt;
but the claim that money gives the right to
monopolize beautiful things of earth, and
the gentle qualities of heart, no longer goes
unchallenged. The culture that is kept close
smells to high heaven: only running water
is pure.

And it is a pleasing fact that although the
men of the Social Exodus lay the blame

all on woman, yet the credit of the return
move must be given to her. Hull House is
primarily woman's work.

"Where is your home?" I asked Miss
Jane Addams a short time ago.

"My home is at Three Hundred Thirty-
five South Halsted Street—my work is
there, and there I expect to live and die,"
was the quiet answer.

🍂 The number of earnest women, highly
cultured in the best sense, who are deeply
interested in social questions, is most encouraging. And when that strong & gentle
woman, Charlotte Perkins Stetson, deliberately casts her lot with the lowly & tells
us that poor people often have a deal more
culture and true charity than we who con-
sider ourselves rich, she voices a truth
that should be passed down the line.

Have your beautiful things, of course—
why not? encourage the workers in art, &
use your money to decorate and beautify,
but do not think that these things will benefit you if you join the Social Exodus and
make hot haste to put distance between
yourself and those who are less fortunate.
Owners of art must build no spite fence !
Show the marbles that fill your niches and

the canvases that glorify your walls to those who seldom see such sights ; give your education to those who need it, your culture to those who have less, & you double your treasure by giving it away.

AS TO THE COUNTRY

THERE is an idea in the minds of many to the effect that the country is an idyllic place to bring up children. Far away from the busy haunts of men, out of the mad rush and tumult, clear of the dust and din of factories, and beyond the reach of vice and depravity—there will we let the little souls fresh from God develop and expand. The singing birds and nodding wild flowers shall be their companions and into their hearts shall be absorbed the sunshine and the sounds that make melody through the branches ● Oho!

I do not wish to appear boastful of our town, but I 'll hazard the challenge that there are a dozen boys hanging around the Railroad Station in East Aurora who can give pointers in depravity and general cussedness to any set of city youngsters you can produce. And East Aurora is far more civilized now than it ever was before.

Last summer a fond mother from Cleveland sent her two sons to an Uncle here, that they might rusticate for a month on the Old Farm and get a healthful glimpse

43

into pastoral life and bucolic ways.♣ They
got it.

One of these boys was ten and the other
twelve years of age. They were not especially brilliant boys, but evidently had receptive minds, for when they got home
their mother soon discovered that they had
mastered the entire Underground Vocabu-
lary of the Rural Deestrick.

The first burst of disillusionment came
when the younger boy, in a proud wish to
show his accomplishments, designated certain necessary functions of life with a pict-
uresque realism that made his mother gasp
for breath, and caused his father to throw
a Double Arab.

In the meantime the elder lad had busied
himself decorating the bath-room after a
hay-mow pattern devised and suggested by
his erstwhile friend, the Hired Man.

This proficiency in art and language caused
the mother to make investigations, and the
result was that she called the laundress and
they stripped those two boys to the buff.
They scrubbed them outside with Pearline,
doped them inside with sulphur, soaped
out their mouths, rubbed Red Precipitate
ointment into their scalps, and burned every

vestige of clothing they had worn on their vacation to the innocent environment of Th' Old Homestead.

East Aurora is not a peculiar place—it is just a plain representative New York State village. New England villages with their libraries & varied industries rank higher, but as you go West, say through Indiana & Illinois, you will find art and letters culti- vated around the railroad stations more assiduously, and vocabularies a trifle more intense.

We have the Hoodlum with us, but not quite so well rounded as the representatives to be seen in the villages of, say, five hun- dred inhabitants, in Ohio.

At present, a stranger arriving here wear- ing a high silk hat would be comparatively safe from mud balls, but a few years ago when an artist came out here sketching, and set up his White Umbrella from Mex- ico in a pasture lot, we pelted his stuck-up circus tent arrangement with stones and set the dogs on him.

This would probably be the fate of any similar presumptuous person in any of the small towns about here, save where the owner of the White Umbrella was a very large man and muscular. The other way to do would be to secure the friendship of some influential citizen in the place who would act as sponsor and body-guard.

Hoodlumism springs naturally into being, like everything else, when the conditions are ripe. The right conditions are idleness and a lack of incentive toward the higher life ✗✗✗

They say people talk gossip in the country, but gossip is only lack of a worthy theme. Having nothing else to talk about, folks turn and talk of each other; and if they rend characters and rip reputations up the back, it is only a sign of mental poverty. Get a man interested in poetry, art, sociology, and he talks of these. Set him to work at some useful employment that calls into being his higher faculties—the love of harmony, proportion, color—and his mind will revolve around these things, and of these will he converse.

Hoodlumism betokens the vacant mind and idle hands. The boy may have glimmering desires to do something useful and be somebody, but he lacks direction—there is none to take lead. He craves excitement, and as the railroad station is the busy center he gravitates there "to see the train come in."

He gets acquainted with the tramps who hang around the water tank and pumping engine room.

Soon he times the Way Freight and curries favor with conductor and brakeman by helping unload boxes, bales and barrels. He learns to climb over freight cars, to set the brake, to board a train in motion.

He is allowed to ride up the road to the next station. He gets off there, and while waiting for a train to take him back, goes over to a farm house & strikes the farmer's wife for a hand-me-out, as he has seen the tramps do ● He gets it.

And lo! it is an epoch in his life—he has learned that he can travel free, and get food without work. At heart he is a tramp and a criminal — he takes something without thought of giving an equivalent.

The next move is by hook, crook and stealth to take the thing without going through the formality of asking for it. If the farmer's wife refuses the food, why just locate the chickens that roost in the trees, and at night go get them!

" The world owes every man a living."

47

In the commodity of manhood, the villages
supply the best and worst. Those with ambition and aspiration seek a field where
their powers can find play; the rest for the
most part hang upon the fringe of hoodlumism 🐝

Governor Rollins of New Hampshire, has
recently lamented the absence of religion in
our rural communities — he says, "the
country towns are drifting into savagery
and hoodlumism for the lack of religion."
Governor Rollins has mental strabismus or
he would know that excitation of the emo-
tional nature is no cure for the disease
which he specifies.

Every hoodlum in East Aurora " comes to
Jesus " every winter. When there is more
excitement at the Baptist Church than there
is at the Railroad Station, the Baptist
Church catches him. And when for a few
weeks his emotions are played upon he
swings off so far in one direction that when
he goes back, as back he must, the mo-
mentum carries him a long way to 't other
side ⬤

The cure for hoodlumism is manual training, and an industrial condition that will
give the boy or girl work—congenial work

48

—a fair wage, and a share in the honors of making things. Salvation lies in the Froebel methods carried into manhood. You encourage the man in well doing by taking the things he makes, the product of hand and brain, and pay him for them, supply a practical, worthy ideal and your hoodlum spirit is gone and gone forever. You have awakened the man to a Higher Life—the life of art and usefulness—you have bound him to his race and made him brother to his kind. The world is larger for him—he is doing something—doing something useful : making things that people want.

All success consists in this : you are doing something for somebody—benefiting humanity; and the feeling of success comes from the consciousness of this.

Interest a person in useful employment and you are transforming Chaos into Cosmos ✦ Blessed is the man who has found his work.

OLD ZEKE CROSBY

OLD ZEKE CROSBY, who as every one knows, lives out on the Mile-Strip, three miles north-west of East Aurora, was down to see me yesterday

Zeke often drops in to make me a friendly call, but the particular thing that brought him this time was my little item about lawyers in a late number of the PHILISTINE. It pleased the old man immensely, and his approval pleased me, for Zeke has a son who is a lawyer— and a good one. The young man, who lives in Chicago, has made a decided success of his profession, and has the confidence of all who know him.

It would have been a very natural pro-ceeding on the part of old Zeke to have denounced my screed on lawyers as libel-ous—and all that. But he did not. On the contrary he had anticipated that my item would bring down on my head a torrent of abuse, not only from the local bar, but from adjacent towns as well.

And so that I might be properly fortified, my friend had, with much labor and great

55

pains, written out his experience with two
Buffalo lawyers.

Old Zeke expects me to print his statement
entire with names and dates, times and
places. And when he reads this I trust he
will pardon me for not doing so, for even
to print the truth is regarded under certain
conditions as libelous. Very briefly stated,
Zeke's complaint No. 1 is that in 1897 he
sold two loads of hay to a Buffalo lawyer,
who is also very well known in East Aurora. Hay was low, only $7.50 a ton, but
he had to sell it in order to get money to
pay taxes ❧

After the hay was delivered the bill was
presented, and the lawyer said he would
mail a check. He has n't mailed the check
yet. Since the hay was sold, hay has been
up to $14.00 a ton.

The lawyer now laughs at Zeke when the
old man asks him for the money, and declares his coachman paid for the hay when
it was delivered.

Case No. 2 is a matter of butter, eggs,
chickens and vegetables supplied to a lawyer's family during a space of two years.
The footings are over three hundred dollars, with seventy-five dollars paid on

56

account. Old Zeke knew the people were rich, and had delayed putting in a bill be- cause he wanted the money all at one time to lift a mortgage. He fully expected it would be paid upon request, but now the bill is repudiated.

They declare the eggs he supplied were bad, the turnips woody, the potatoes rotten & that all of his spring chickens were hens old enough to vote. When the old man attempted to defend his good name he was ordered from the premises, and soundly abused by the lawyer's wife. On refusing to go the woman rang for a stable-man and ordered the man-servant to kick Old Zeke into the street. The hostler took Zeke by the arm and induced him to go, and when in the alley, he gave the old man a dollar out of his own pocket, apologizing for his share in the matter, and declared by way of extenuation, that he just had to make a show of pulling Old Zeke out or lose his job.

Well, what does all this prove? Nothing at all, save that two men, who are accidentally lawyers, have treated a generous and kindly old man with gross injustice. Lawyers are not all bad and all dead-beats are not lawyers, but some lawyers are

rogues and all lawyers are officers of the
Court — servants of the Goddess, who,
being blind, never sees anything of their
rascality ☙

To us who are young and tough and mix-
ing in the world, Old Zeke's troubles all
seem slight and trivial.

If I should print the names and pedigree of
that family on Delaware Avenue, Buffalo,
N. Y., who were fed by this old farmer for
two years, and who then turned upon him
and abused him cruelly, it would not secure
his money. And should I go with St. Ge-
rome-Roycroft and play rough-house with
their kitchen, do up the servants, black the
eyes of the Honest Lawyer, and scare the
Lady of the House into hysterics, it would
do no good, and the Saint and I might get
six months apiece for interesting ourselves
in matters that are none of ours.

Well, it does n't make much difference!
Let the great lawyer who owes Zeke for
two loads of hay laugh the old man into
babbling embarrassment; and let the proud
Lady of the House who has taken on un-
due adipose at his expense screech at him
that "he is a nasty old thing." Who
cares!

The old man has passed his three score & ten—he is living only by God's grace. His children are all grown up and gone—his work is done. Let him go home to his weed-covered farm and tell his old wife his troubles, and together let them cry salt tears down their wrinkled cheeks—it won't help their failing eyesight any, I tell you that. Who cares? The neighbors will come in before long, and then go down town and send telegrams to Chicago, Des Moines and Cleveland, and in three days they will form a procession and head for the cemetery.

I 'm not sure just what the unpardonable sin is, but I believe it is the disposition to evade the payment of small bills.

The folks who abused Old Zeke Crosby are not "bad" people. On the contrary they move in the best circles of society, belong to the Presbyterian Church, and are eminently respectable. They lack imagination, for if they could understand the misery, the worry and the pain they cause, it is not at all probable they would inflict it. They fire the farmer out—& forget him. To them, that is all there is of it.

59

Now if they are unjust to a helpless old
farmer, they are also unjust to others.
Doubtless dressmakers, grocers, butchers
and other plain people suffer at their hands
in the same way. Their lives are so full
looking after the mere machinery of life—
so filled with selfishness, that they ride
right over other folks, and no matter how
many are crushed beneath the wheels of
their chariots, they know nothing of it. Yet
they go "slumming," belong to mission-
ary societies and contribute to College
Settlements ✗✗✗
Does not "Society" in its society sense
breed just this dead, cruel, thoughtless
indifference ? It does seem so, for even in
our little town the only dead-beats are those
who are in the "set." Ask the grocer, the
livery-man, or the butcher who are the
folks that contract bills and never pay, or
pay whenever they please, and he will tell
you they are the aristocrats. The carpen-
ters, stone-masons, blacksmiths & farmers
look you squarely in the eye, speak to you
frankly face to face, and if they promise to
pay you Saturday night, and cannot, they
come around and tell you why. I have been
despoiled of hard-earned dollars, and had

60

my reputation ripped up the back when
I ventured to ask for my own, but never
excepting by those who have a Thursday.
● If you wish to lessen the worries of the
world and scatter sunshine as you go, do n't
bother to go a-slumming, or lift the fallen,
or trouble to reclaim the erring—simply
pay your debts cheerfully and promptly. It
lubricates the wheels of trade, breaks up
party ice, gives tone to the social system
and liberates good-will.

Pay as you go.

Especially pay the people who work by the
day and toil with their hands. A dollar
means much to the man who spades your
garden—never humiliate the man by making him ask for his dollar ● Give it to him
immediately the work is done, and if he
did well, tell him so. When the woman
who crouches over a sewing machine for
you, all day long, brings the garment home,
pay her all you owe, and do not add to her
troubles by exercising the prerogative of
the one who is paying over money, to
flaunt out either insulting remarks or insulting manners.

The Gentle Man shows his true nature in
his treatment of social inferiors; and of all

61

A MESSAGE TO GARCIA damning sins, the withholding of money due a working man is the worst. Let us pay as we go. And the cheerfulness and good-will we give out with our money will in turn be given out by those we pay it to. Pay as you go.

THE BROTHERHOOD
OF JINERS

N O, I do not belong to a Church nor to any Secret Society.
I do not belong to anything, except the East Aurora Hook and Ladder Company.

Why should any one who is free, belong? ● Of course I am a member of the Society of the Philistines, but as I can resign at any time if there appears an item in the Magazine I do not like, it cannot be said that I really belong. To belong implies that some one has a rope fastened to your foot. And furthermore, I do not want any one to "belong" to me.
I would hold my friend only by the virtue that is in me — by the attraction of the worth that is in my soul.
Still, I might belong to a Secret Society if there was wisdom to be gained thereby that could not be gotten in any other way.
But mark you this, Dearie, there is no Secret Society that has corralled truth. Truth is in the air, and when your head gets into the right stratum you know it. No one can impart it to you until the time is ripe, and when the time is ripe for you to know, you

67

do not have to ride a Goat in order to understand. God's Eternal Truth is not to be secured that way.

Darwin says the herding instinct in animals has its base in fear.

Sheep and cattle go in droves, while a lion simply flocks with his mate—and lets it go at that. Frederick Nietzsche writes in his Third Essay on the "Genealogy of Morals," " Prompted by a desire to cast off depression and impotence, the sickly and weak instinctively strive for gregarious organization. Those who wish to lead have always fostered fear, encouraging this tendency to herd, promising protection and offering to impart valuable knowledge in return for a luxurious livelihood."

The Jiner instinct in man is a manifestation of weakness, not strength. It is a clutch to get something for nothing, a grab at good which you have not earned.

By going with a gang you hope to grow wise ♣ But while wisdom has sometimes come to men in solitude, it is not to be found in the crowd. I am opposed on principle to secrets. Is truth a thing to hide in a ginger jar on a high shelf? You are welcome to all the good I can impart, and if

you are in possession of truth that the
world needs and you keep it back, you are
not my kind ✣

But the fact is, you can't. In years agone,
when every man's hand was against his
neighbor, it was proper and right for men
to unite with other men in order to stand
against a common foe. Clan fought clan
with tooth and nail, and to despoil and rob
and kill was the right of him who could—
and to further this sort of thing, Secret
Societies with their shibboleths and pass-
words and signs and grips came into being.
Secret Societies are a product of savagery,
and the fact that they exist is proof of our
origin. All men are my brothers, not just
those who belong.

Of course I do not claim that Secret Societies are savage institutions now. On the
contrary they are quite toothless, innocent
affairs where men meet for frolic and good
fellowship. As social institutions they are
all right; but bless your soul! they have
no "secrets."

The answer to that last remark, I know full
well is, "How do you know, since you do
not belong?" ✣

And so I will say, well, I know the men

who do. They are pretty good fellows, too. One of them who has attained the 48th Degree in Something owns the farm next to mine, and in summer we often go swimming together in the creek. When we stand upon the bank, stripped, ready to dive off into th' ole swimmin' hole, I 'll defy Herr Tuefelsdroch, or any of his Disciples, to tell which biped holds in his epidermis the Great Secret Doctrine.

Does my neighbor possess Spiritual Truth that I do not ?

No, Dearie ☛ He is a nice man, but he is not in possession of any great South African Spiritual gems. If he were it would make him round-shouldered to carry them. And the virtue of my neighbor lies in the fact that when we are alone together, he confesses that all his jining has given him no insight into the Mystery of Things. He jines out of pure sociability.

Then there are various other worthy men in town who belong to Lodges. I know two dozen of them or more. I have known some of them for twenty years, and have been with them under every vicissitude of life. I buy oats and hay of them ; and when they bring me potatoes the scrubby ones are often in the bottom of the bag. I meet these Jiners at the Grocery, or the Station when we go down to see the four-o'clock train come in; I often pitch horse shoes with them, and surely I would be base to insinuate that anything was wrong in their Secret Society doin's.

All the point I wish to make is that they are not much beyond me in esoteric truth, for I usually turn the bag of tubers out on the barn floor before I make a price on them. One reason why I criticise Secret Societies is that they, for the most part, exclude women. If a thing is good, the man who would hide it away from the woman he loves is only a 2 x 4; and if a thing is no good and he pretends to Her it is, & keeps it on a high shelf, he is still a 2 x 4—and both are aware of it.

Very much has been said by the Funny Press about attending Lodge and the consequent marital infelicity that sometimes follows; but the joke is founded on a very grim and lamentable fact. Secret Societies tend to separate the sexes in their mental occupations, and this is the most grievous count that can be brought against them. Men and women should commune intellectually: to lovey-dovey is not enough. Only to lovey-dovey is to hate afterwards. Where men & women meet only to lovey-dovey, society is essentially barbaric; and where the males monopolize, or think, or pretend to think, that they monopolize wisdom, there is small hope for progress. Man cannot advance and leave woman behind. And the one point of congratulation in this whole Secret Society business is that Secret Societies have no secrets that are worth a tuppenny dam. The wisdom that is among them is free to any man or woman who can absorb it ❦

I have met a few men and women in my lifetime who were in possession of valuable Spiritual Truth. And I knew it, not from what they said, but because there shone from their faces a light, and from their persons there went a radiance, and in all their actions was a dignity that gave their words weight ● But these rare beings did not "belong"—they were themselves, and they were great because they were. Into their souls there had been absorbed a goodly meed of the Divine Spirit ❧ Let's keep the windows open to the East, be worthy, and sometime we shall know.

72

ABOUT ADVERTISING
BOOKS

NE of the mysteries of this world is why one book will reach a sale of a hundred thousand copies and another one equally good falls flat. There was "Ships that pass in the Night" that out-sold any book of its day—gone now, like ships that pass in the night. It was n't a bad book, nor so very good; just such as five hundred girls who have had their souls quickened, and wits sharpened, and hearts bruised by a little Experience, write every year. Books like that are written hot off the bat, as my friend Mr. Dooley would say. And all good things are so written, although, of course, it would be a mistake to assume that all things so written are good. Yet the presses of a dozen publishers ran overtime and could not supply the demand for Beatrice Harraden's book ✕✕✕✕

Well, what sold it? Newspaper advertising? No, dearie, newspaper advertising does not sell books; newspaper advertising sells some things, but not books. To simply announce that you have Soulheaver's poems may be good policy, for possibly some one

77

is looking for Soulheaver's works, but no
amount of praise added to your advertisement will cause a stranger to invest in
Soulheaver. Columns of puffery by paid
"reviewers" do not sell books. I 've had
a paper with a hundred thousand circula-
tion give one of my books a lavish write-up
of a full column, and the stuff did not fetch
a single order.

On the other hand, a few weeks ago I
received six orders in one day for a book
from the comparatively obscure town of
Humboldt, Iowa, and all were traceable to
a certain young woman who read from the
volume at a teacher's convention.

It seems this young woman had the confidence and respect and affection of her
auditors ❧ Her recommendation carried
weight. When she said, "I hold in my
hand a book; it is so good that I want you
to enjoy it with me," immediately there
was a desire in the hearts of several in that
little audience to own a copy of that iden-
tical book; for that which could minister to
the wants of this strong, discriminating,
yet gentle girl, they felt must be worth
while. These kind folk who bought my
book, because a Discerning young woman

78

recommended it, in their turn sold a hundred copies. They possibly were not aware
of it—but they did.

There is a fellow by the name of William Hawley Smith, who could play Cyrano de Bergerac without an artificial beak, but whose generous heart is so big that his nose is an insignificant pug in proportion. He, too, could fight & compose a ballad at the same time, pinking you at the l' envoi.

When Hawley Smith and Zangwill met in Chicago, the Dreamer of the Ghetto fell on the neck of Smith, cried for joy, and exclaimed, "At last! Thank God, I 've found a man as homely as myself!"

Hawley Smith has analyzed the problem of education as thoroughly as did Jean Jacques Rousseau and practiced it a deal better; and if he had not allowed his compass to go off ten points in deference to the Methodist Church, would have written as deathlessly. But had he written as well as he could, like Jean Jacques, he might have asked for bread and been given a pile of stone—after he was dead.

Hawley, he once read from one of my books and simply told the audience that in his opinion the work was not so bad as it

might be, and the next day every book-
dealer in that town was wiring Putnam's
Sons to "Send by first Express," etc. This
shows how some folks regard Hawley
Smith's opinions.

The Sons wrote to me asking if I had been
out blowing my Horn. I replied, "No, and
even if I had it would have made no special difference in sales—it 's all the fault of
de Bergerac Smith."

The Sons replied by wire, "Engage Bergerac ten years contract his own terms." 🐟
By the way, Hawley Smith wrote a book
that has sold well over a hundred thousand
copies, and has done more to evolve education in America into common-sense lines
than anything Pestalozzi ever printed. This
little book has been a world-mover—I will
not tell you its title—you are to be pitied if
you do not know it—and yet the author
never got a dollar out of it. When he wrote
it, publishers sniffed at it, others mocked,
one took it as a gift and told the author he
was welcome to look in the show windows
whenever he passed by, and all the icicles
on the cornice were his if he cared to climb
up and get them 🦋

But let us go back, ere we stray, and say,

Bergerac could not be hired to boom books;
and if he could, his recommendation would
be worthless ✿ His word is only valuable
because it is not for sale. The advertisement
that secures recognition and really sells the
book cannot be purchased—it cannot even
be asked for—but must spring spontaneous
from the sympathetic heart. To request it
would be to lose it, for like love, it goes to
him who does not ask for it, and passes in
silence all those who plot, scheme and lie
in wait. It goes only to the worthy: but
alas! the worthy sometimes—aye, often,
pine away of heart-hunger, and there is no
hand to caress, nor gentle voice to soothe;
and youth flies fast, and recognition comes
only when it is no more desired, and when
the presence of cool, all-enfolding death—
strong deliveress—is more grateful than
the applause of men.

✿ Good horseshoe nails are always good
nails, but what is good in literature is all a
matter of taste. There is no standard. You
like it because you like it, and if certain
other people praise a thing it is a good reason why you should let it severely alone—
or buy it. It all depends upon who this
person is ✿.

When you read a column of unsigned puffery in the "Tribune" about Jingle's latest novel, you are not influenced in Jingle's favor even in the estimation of a hair, for you do not know the writer ✼ If the reviewer's style is bad, or you think it is, you probably inwardly vow you will never read Jingle under any conditions, because Jingle has pleased a man of bad taste, and this is a fit excuse for eschewing Jingle ♣ In advertising a book I would rather quote the reviewers who damned it, than those who were lavish in their praise. Books well damned often boom, but books merely praised in print—bah! Who wants 'em? When a book is damned in print the damnation is sincere, but fulsome flattery is usually the work of some fellow who never read the volume—and all prospective buyers know it. Unscathing criticism of a work indicates that it is a Bible to some, and thus are averages held good.

My own ambition is to write a book that will be excluded from the mails; and then my fortune will be made. If John Wanamaker again comes into power, I think I can fetch it ✼✼

A book booms in the market, usually because one friend recommends it to another. No person can read a book secretly and by stealth, and then gloat over it alone ❧ A woman may discover the only pure baking powder and chuckle over her rich find— keeping the secret to herself so as to make other housewives envious of her biscuit, but she can never read a book and like it (or dislike it) and keep the fact to herself. All book lovers have chums, and the pleasure of reading is to pass this joy along to another. Lovers always read together, and the chief joy of loving a woman is to read to her, or have her read to you. To mix it mentally with a good woman who has phosphorous, is paradise enow.

Books that have boomed have usually been those that have been spurned by publishers and gone a-begging, and yet publishers are often very shrewd men. The sale started, nobody knows just how. The only book I have mentioned by name in this article was thought so little of by publisher and author that it was n't even copyrighted, and to name others that have boomed in spite of publishers would be merely to deal in the tritest kind of truism. Cast about in your mind and recall incidents

83

to suit ◆ No advertiser has ever had the
talent to force a thoroughly bad book upon
the market and make it sell. Ten thousand
dollars invested in newspaper advertising
will start an inquiry for any nostrum or
brand of goods, but a moribund book can
never be galvanized into life.

What men call "luck" or "chance" is the
result of law not understood. And the luck
that makes a book "go" is regulated by a
law that no advertising expert has yet been
able to control. Mystery enshrouds it all.
The man who by his genius can blow
this mist away and place his hand
upon the law that controls the
popularity of a good book,
shall have riches and
honor and undy-
ing renown.

CONSECRATED LIVES

HERE's a thought, Dearie, that I give to you because I have n't a very firm grasp upon it myself. In order to clarify my mind I explain to you ❧ And thus, probably, do I give you something which is already yours. Grateful? of course you are —there! ❧❧

The thought is this:—but before I explain it let me tell of what a man saw in a certain cottage in Denmark. And it was such a little white-washed cottage, too, with a single, solitary rose bush clambering over the door! An Artist, his Wife and their Little Girl lived there. There were four rooms, only, in this cottage—a kitchen, a bedroom, a workroom & the Other Room. The kitchen was for cooking, the bedroom for sleeping, the workroom for work, and the Other Room was where the occupants of the cottage received their few visitors. When the visitors remained for tea or lunch the table was spread in the Other Room, but usually the Artist, his Wife and their Little Girl ate their meals in the kitchen, or in summer on the porch at the back of

the house ✐✐ Now the Artist painted pic-
tures, and his Wife carved beautiful shapes
in wood ; but they did n't make much
money—in fact no one seemed to know
them, at all. They did n't have funds to
accumulate a library, and perhaps would
not if they had. But still they owned all
the books written by Georg Brandes.
These books were kept in a curious little
case, which the Artist and his Wife, themselves, had made.
✐ And before the case of books was an
ancient Roman lamp, suspended from the
ceiling by a chain.
And the lamp was kept always lighted,
night and day.
Each morning, before they tasted food, the
man & his Wife read from Georg Brandes,
and then they silently refilled, trimmed &
made the lamp all clean and tidy.
Oho ! why, your eyes are filling with tears
—how absurd—& you want to hear more
about the Artist and his Wife and the
Little Girl !
But, bless me ! that is all I know about
them ✐✐
However, I do know that Georg Brandes
is one of the Apostles of the Better Day.

His message is a plea for beauty—that is
to . say, harmony ✍ He would have us
live lives of simplicity, truth, honesty and
gentleness. He would have us work for
harmony and love, instead of for place and
power. Georg Brandes is an individualist
and a symbolist. He thinks all of our be-
longings should mean much to us, and that
great care should be exercised in selection.
We need only a few things, but each of
these things should suggest utility, strength,
harmony and truth ✍ All of our actions
must be suggestive of peace and right. Not
only must we speak truth, but we must
live it. Our lives should be consecrated to
the good—lives consecrated to Truth and
Beauty. Consecrated Lives!
And so this Artist and his Wife, I told you
of were priests of Beauty, and their little
girl was a neophyte; and the room where
the Roman lamp burned was filled with
the holiness of beauty, and no unkind
thought or wrong intent could exist there.
✍ Consecrated Lives! that is the subject.
There is a brotherhood of such, and you
can reach out and touch finger tips with
the members the round world over ✍ ✍
Beauty is an Unseen Reality—an attempt

to reveal a spiritual condition. Members of this Brotherhood of Consecrated Lives do not take much interest in Salisbury's Political Policy, and all the blatant blowing of brass horns that are used on 'Change, in pulpits, or by Fourth of July speakers are to them trivial and childish. They distinguish at once the note of affectation, hypocrisy & pretense in it all. They know its shallowness, its selfishness and its extremely transient quality.

Yet your man of the Consecrated Life may mix with the world, and do the world's business, but for him it is not the true world, for hidden away in his heart he keeps burning a lamp before a shrine dedicated to Love & Beauty. The Adept only converses at his best with Adept, and he does this through self-protection. To hear the world's coarse laugh in his Holy of Holies—no! and so around him is a sacred circle, and within it only the Elect are allowed to enter.

To join this brotherhood of Consecrated Lives requires no particular rites of initiation—no ceremonial—no recommendations. You belong when you are worthy. ☛ But do not for a moment imagine you have solved the difficulty when you have once entered. To pride yourself on your entrance is to run the danger of finding yourself outside the pale with password hopelessly forgotten. Within the esoteric lines are circles and inner circles, and no man yet has entered the inmost circle where the Ark of the Covenant is secreted. All is relative ✍✍

But you know you belong to the Brotherhood when you feel the absolute nothingness of this world of society, churches, fashion, politics and business; and realize strongly the consciousness of the Unseen World of Truth, Love and Beauty. The first emotion on coming into the Brotherhood is one of loneliness & isolation. You pray for comradeship, & empty arms reach out into the darkness. But gradually you awaken to the thought that you are one of many who hope and pray alike; and that slowly this oneness of thought and feeling is making its impress felt.

Then occasionally you meet one of your own. This one may be socially high or low, rich or poor, young or old, man or woman—but you recognize each other on sight and hold sweet converse. Then you

93

part, mayhap, never to meet again, but you are each better, stronger, nobler for the meeting 🌿🌿

Consecrated Lives! You meet & you part, but you each feel a firmer impulse to keep the light burning—the altar light to Truth, Simplicity and Beauty. No other bond is required than that of devotion to Truth, the passion of listening in the Silence, the prayer for Wholeness and Harmony, the earnest desire to have your life reflect the Good 🌿🌿

All man-made organization would be fatal to the sweet, subtle and spiritual qualities of the Brotherhood 🌿 For organization means officers, judicial robes, livery, arbitrary differentiation, and all the vile and foolish clap-trap of place and power. It means the wish to dictate, select & exclude, and this means jealousy, prejudice and bitterness—fifteen candidates for a vacant bishopric with heart-aches to match! 🌿 No organization ever contained within its ranks the best. Organization is arbitrary and artificial! it is born of selfishness; and at the best is a mere matter of expediency. 🌿 The Brotherhood of Consecrated Lives admits all who are worthy, and all who

94

are excluded, exclude themselves. If your
Life is to be a genuine consecration, you
must be free. Only the free man is truthful;
only the heart that is free is pure. How
many compose this Brotherhood—who
shall say? There are no braggart statisti-
cians, no paid proselytes with their noisy
boastings. Two constitute a congregation
and where they commune is a temple.
Many belong who do not know it; others
there be who think they belong, and are so
sure of it that they do not.
But the Brotherhood is extending its lines;
and what think you the earth will be like
when the majority of men and women
in it learn that to be simple and
honest and true, is the part of
wisdom, & that to work
for Love & Beauty is
the highest good?

95

THE BEECHAM
HABIT

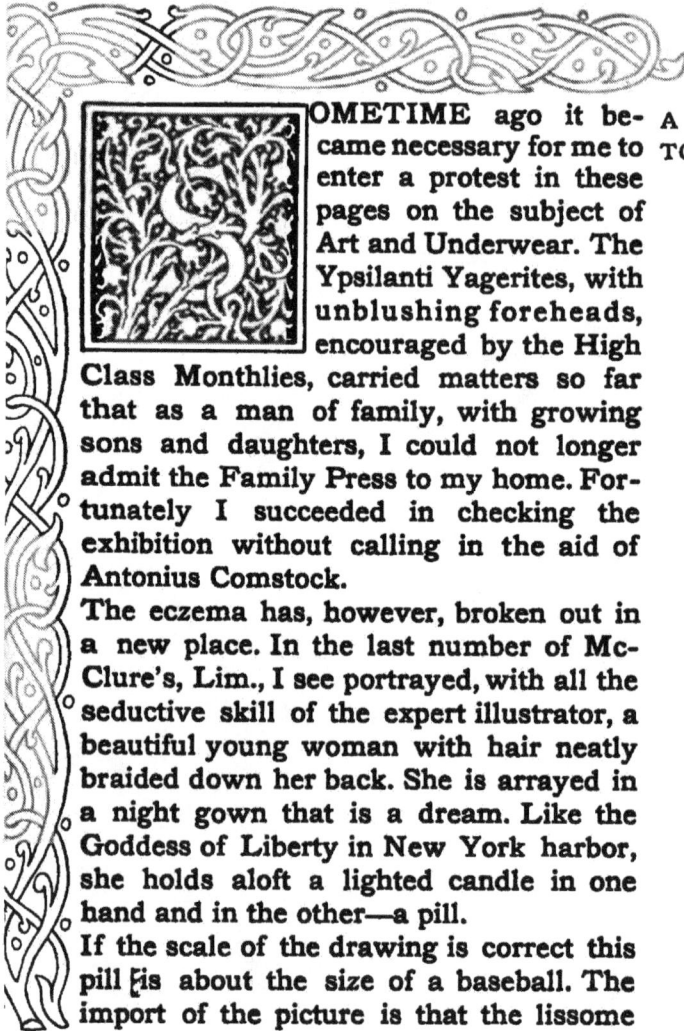

OMETIME ago it be-
came necessary for me to
enter a protest in these
pages on the subject of
Art and Underwear. The
Ypsilanti Yagerites, with
unblushing foreheads,
encouraged by the High
Class Monthlies, carried matters so far
that as a man of family, with growing
sons and daughters, I could not longer
admit the Family Press to my home. For-
tunately I succeeded in checking the
exhibition without calling in the aid of
Antonius Comstock.

The eczema has, however, broken out in
a new place. In the last number of Mc-
Clure's, Lim., I see portrayed, with all the
seductive skill of the expert illustrator, a
beautiful young woman with hair neatly
braided down her back. She is arrayed in
a night gown that is a dream. Like the
Goddess of Liberty in New York harbor,
she holds aloft a lighted candle in one
hand and in the other—a pill.

If the scale of the drawing is correct this
pill [is about the size of a baseball. The
import of the picture is that the lissome

beauty is about to swallow the baseball. Beneath the picture is the legend: "My complexion is perfect because I take one of Billson's Bully Bilious Boluses every night on retiring."

Now, not only do I solemnly protest against this realistic tendency in art on the part of Billson, but I call attention to some truths brought to my notice by the ship's doctor on the " Lucania." This doctor, who seems to Understand Himself, declares the Beecham Habit is very much on the increase. He says that the people who insist on irritating their Erie Canal by doses of the invention of Colonel Carter, of Cartersville, as soon as they come on board are sure to pay speedy tribute to Neptune in a surprising and unexpected way, & that those addicted to the Beecham Habit are the ones that suffer most when traveling on the sad sea waves.

The Family Papers teem with warnings that we must invest good money in Fig Syrup, Early Risers, Little Liver Pills and Base Ball Boluses in order to have good complexions and sweet thoughts. Very many people believe this. The habit begins by gentle dallyings with the Lady

Webster Dinner Pill. It grows and grows.
One pill is enough at first, but two are
soon required where only one grew before,
then three are demanded, and soon a
change is required from Pills to Fig Syrup,
then Mother Shipley's Tea and back to
Pills — from Carter's to Pierce's, then
Ayer's, Beecham's, Billson's, and at last a
frantic dash is made for Ripum's Tablets.
⚓ The man's hold has been stored with
such a miscellaneous cargo that Nature
stops perplexed; Carter is consulted, and
she starts, she moves, she seems to feel
the thrill of life along her keel. Then come
cold chills, hot bearings, a hawser has
surely befouled the screw. Stomach pro-
tests—mal de mer comes ashore—liver
lags, kidneys kick, lee scuppers are clogged,
bilge accumulates and Nature pipes all
hands to pump ship.
The patient goes into dry dock and spec-
ialists being consulted tell him he has can-
cer of the stomach, fistula, appendicitis,
tape worm, tuberculosis of the bowels and
Bright's disease, and he has, or thinks he
has—which is just as bad.
And all this as a result of the Beecham
Habit. It is very plain to every unpreju-

103

diced reader that the prime motive of the
fin de siecle Religious Press is to prove
that man has liver trouble and salvation
can only be found by patronizing Dr.
Pierce's Pungent, Pugnacious, Pollywog
Perquisites 🖋
Whether these things be dictated by Bishop, Presbytery, or Ecumenical Council, I
cannot say. But Colonel George Batten,
Expert in Advertising, advises me that the
proper cathartic is usually dictated by the
Committee of Seventy. However this is, I
find that the "Outlook" gives prominence
and publicity to Tarrant's Seltzer, the
"Churchman" to Fig Syrup, the "Christian Register" to Acid Phosphate, while
strong leanings are shown by the "Christian Leader" for the wares of Dr. Pierce.
"The Christian at Work" works Pierce
and Ayer, the "Presbyterian" likes Prune
Juice, while the "Christian Advocate"
lustily advocates Early Risers and Ripum's Tablets. The "Baptist Standard"
goes off on a new track and favors Dr.
Hall's Water Cure Self-Treatment, while
the "Examiner" falls back to Fig Syrup
and Prunes. The "Christian Herald,'
edited by Rev. Dr. Talmage, seems to

conduct itself rather loosely, for it co-
quettes its favors between Hood, Beecham
and Dr. Hall. As one goes south of the
Ohio River, matters grow worse, for the
" Southern Pulpit" of Louisville not only
favors Pierce, Carter and Beecham, but
introduces " a sure cure for flatulence," in
the presence of one Doctor Jingle, whose
wares are vouched for by seven clergymen,
three of them D. D.'s.
The opinion is well grounded among our
agrarian population that the chief claim
of our late martyred President upon the
gratitude of a loving public lies in the fact
that he invented Garfield Tea.
Not long since in a court of law Fig Syrup
was acknowledged to be innocent of Figs.
And gentlemen having purchased Prune
Extract and congratulating themselves
that they are full of prunes have only taken
a drastic dose of aloes.
It seems the part of wisdom for those on
sea (and land) to monkey with their in'ards
as little as possible. One's motto in this
respect should be, " Place not your trust in
prophylactics." It is difficult to improve on
the plans of God. Many men have tried it,
but to their sorrow ✒ He has made all

out-of-doors full of fresh air. He gives us
pleasure in moderate exercise, the night
for sleep, and fruit drops from the trees at
our feet. All these He made and I hardly
think He ever intended that we should
put an enemy into our mouths to steal
away our digestion—still, I may be wrong.

THE BISHOP'S
VOICE

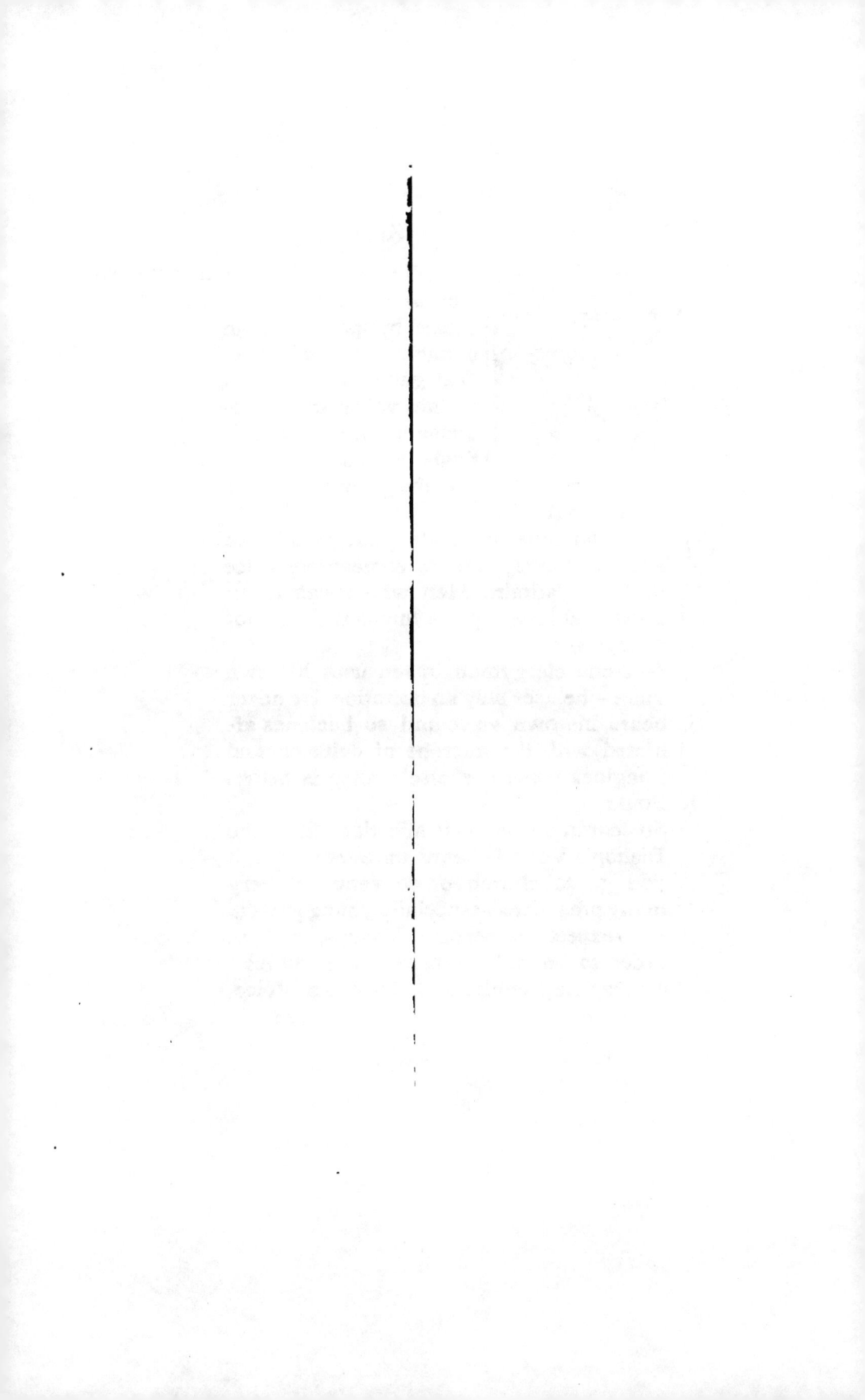

LERGYMEN'S Sore
Throat or Tonsilitis is
caused by speaking in an
unnatural tone of voice.
God gave each of us a
certain voice, and to ex-
ercise it wisely and cul-
tivate it is good.

The voice should be the sounding-board
of the soul.

But you must cultivate your own voice
and not merely imitate some other voice
that you admire. Men who speak in an
unnatural tone express things they do not
believe ❦ ❦

Not one clergyman in ten uses his own
voice—he uses only an imitation. He never
hears his own voice and so becomes afflicted with the microbe of delusion and
imagines some one else's voice is better.
Pouf!

So common is this affection that the
Bishop's Voice is heard on every hand, if
you go to church or conventions. Very
many preachers—especially young preachers—expect to become bishops, and in
order to be fully prepared when the call
comes, they cultivate a Bishop's Voice.

All bishops are supposed to be powerful and lusty, also full of besum. Therefore it is imagined that they have voices like bulls of Bashan. When they pray they shake the rafters of Heaven.

Beware of the Bishop's Voice—your own is better ✿✿

Actors who cultivate the Brutus, Virginius and Sardanapalus voice and preachers who use the Bishop's Voice are fit candidates for vegetables. Worse than that— they are candidates for tonsilitis, simply because they are abusing the physical organs of speech.

Worse than that—they are candidates for Nervous Prostration, because they have ceased to be themselves and are trying to pass for someone else.

Worse than that—they are losing their own souls, because they are not allowing a true exercise and expression of their Inner Spirit.

Americanitis, Nervous Exhaustion and Mental Prostration—one and the same thing—is the result of trying to pass for something different from what you are. Men who try to conceal their own voice and praise God with the Bishop's Bazoo

112

are in danger ❧ Concealment is friction.
A secret gnaws.
To religiously observe the Twelfth Commandment, "Thou shalt not be found out," leads to loss of manhood, cold feet, that tired feeling, premature decay and the surgeon's knife.

To love is very beautiful—but to feel you must conceal and hide and refute and deny your Saviour before men is terrible. If you use language to conceal your thought you better begin taking hypophosphites, for you are breaking down tissue faster than Nature can build it up. God only calculates on each man being himself, and the presumption originally was that he would be honest. You see it is like this— the Universe is not planned for duplicity. ❧ To carry a live fox around under your bellyband will interfere sooner or later with your digestive apparatus.

The Roberts plan is a thousand times better than the Breckinridge—ask Breckinridge! Long, long years ago God blessed the Roberts copyright, although I am told He has since changed His mind, but He placed his curse upon the Mr. Hyde and Dr. Jekyll business right from the start, and the embargo has never been removed. The Double-Life does not go. Don't be a fool, Lambert of Indiana—the sin is in affectation, concealment, subterfuge, crying, sneaking, cringing, denying. Don't you know that?

Be yourself. Have nothing to conceal.

To hell with the Bishop's Voice.

Carry the fox no longer—he wants liberty as much as you.

———

You shall know the worst about me. It is not all sweet and savory, but if you want to know I'll tell you. I used to have headache, bad breath, sore throat, watery eyes, night sweats and buzzing sounds in the ears; but since I took the pledge that I would just simply be myself, live my own life, one day at a time, I have gained twenty pounds in weight; sleep eight hours without waking; eat anything in sight; and have the limit to my credit in four Savings Banks.

P. S. I cheerfully recommend God's Remedies, and will send my picture, before and after using, to all the afflicted who may apply ✍

114

THE KINDERGARTEN
OF GOD

EAR Playmate in the Kindergarten of God: Please do not take life quite so seriously—you surely will never get out of it alive. And as for your buying and selling, your churches & banks, your newspapers and books, they are really at the last of no more importance than the child's paper houses, red and blue wafers and funny scissors things. Why you grown-ups! all your possessions are only just to keep you out of mischief, until Death, the good old nurse, comes & rocks you to sleep. Am I not right?

The child's paper doll lasts a day and a copy of a daily paper lasts only half a day or until the next edition appears; and as for a church edifice it only endures for two days, if made of wood, and three if of stone. In Egypt I saw men unearthing stone temples, and no one really knows what god these temples were dedicated to, much less why. The god they sought to serve is as dead as the folks who invented him ✍ ✍

Take my word for it, Dear Playmate, this

119

life is only a big joke. But we are here,
and so let's have all the fun we can. And
in order to get along best we should cut
our scissors things as well as we can, and
model only pretty toys out of the mud that
is given us. It's all Kindergarten business
though : the object is to teach us. I really
believe we are learning things, and if we
are ever called to a Higher Grade we
shall be prepared to manage more difficult lessons than when we began here.

We are all children in the Kindergarten of
God. Take my word for it, Playmate, and
I know as much about God and his plans
as any man who ever trod this green
earth. I know as much as you, and you
know as much as I, and we are both Sons
of God and it doth not yet appear what
we shall be ✒

Systems of Guesswork, facetiously called
" Theology," do not introduce us to God.
Theologians are absurd men with high-
cut vests and bishop's voices. Learned
men—professors of Christology, praters
on Homiletics, writers of Syllogistic essays
and such, have confounded and confused
men and covered truth with their brush-
piles of words. These men with many

sharked up reasons are bad angels, and the wind of their wings withers as it passes. Their efforts have all tended to befog and blind, while the Seers and Prophets and Poets and Doers have endeavored to simplify ⚓

"Do unto others as you would be done by "—you understand that, do you not? But what does a man mean when he talks of Predestination, Vicarious Atonement, Redemption by Faith and Hell and Damnation?

Please take my word for it when I say these schemes of salvation are as idle vapors; for I am a Son of God, and most of the preachers who preach their little "schemes" are children of the Devil, born in sin, and admit it.

I am a thought of God; I was loved into being, therefore my life in the beginning was holy. Of course I am slightly besmirched by contact with fools, but in the main my life and deeds are right, for being a Child of God I could not stray very far afield, even if I wished; God, who is my mother, would call me back, for has He not protected me, sustained me and cared for me all these years? Take my

word for it, we are in the Kindergarten of
God, and all there is of life is to do our
work (which is only play) as well as we
can and be kind. That's all there is of
wisdom—do your work as well as you can
and be kind *

I know as much about it as any man who
ever lived, for I am a Child of God, and
the best man who ever lived was nothing
more. Do your work as well as you can
and be kind—that's the best way to get
along here, and it is the best preparation
for a Life to Come, if there is one. This is
no new Truth, for there is no such thing
as a new Truth. Truth is as old as Fate.
There is no plural Truth—there is only the
one Truth, and this is very old and very
simple. All wise men have known it. No
one knows any more about Absolute
Truth than I do, and I know as
much about it as anyone who
ever lived, and I know
nothing * Do your
work as well as you
can and be kind.

ADVANTAGES AND DISADVANTAGES

THE so-called "disadvantages" in the life of a child are often its advantages. And on the other hand "advantages" are very often disadvantages of a most serious sort. To be born in the country, of poor parents, is no disadvantage. The strong men in every American city—the men who can do things; the men like James J. Hill, Charles E. Perkins, Philip G. Armour, Norton Finney, S. S. Merrill, or the late Tom Potter, who gloried in difficulties, waxed strong in overcoming obstacles & laughed at disaster—men who could build three miles of railroad a day, and cause prosperous cities to spring up where before were only swamps and jungle, barren plains or endless forest—these men were all country boys, nurtured in adversity ✒ And it is but the tritest truism to say that the early life of industry and unceasing economy of time and things, was the best possible preparation and education that these men could have had for doing a great work ✒

127

I once heard George M. Pullman tell how at ten years of age he used to cut wood so his mother could cook, help her wash the dishes and sweep; carry water for her to do the washing, and assist her hanging out the clothes. In a year or two more he planted the garden, knew all kinds of vegetable seeds on sight, knew every forest tree that grew in Western New York and could distinguish between the qualities of the wood. At seventeen he helped his father move houses and barns and dig wells and construct church steeples. That is to say he was getting an education—learning to do things in the best way. He was developing physique and also building character and making soul-fibre. He was learning to make plans and execute them, think for himself and be strong and self-reliant. Yet he did n't know it at the time, and later regretted his lack of education and absence of opportunity.

Pullman was always a little too busy to be a philosopher; in spite of his mighty grasp on practical things he failed to perceive that he was a product of the " unkind conditions" of his boyhood. He plumed himself on overcoming great difficulties.

In after dinner conferences he occasionally recited the great things he had done and compared them to the still greater things he might have done "if he had only had a chance."

Perhaps George M. Pullman knew down deep in his heart that he had received the very best training possible for his life work; but that quality in "self-made" men which causes them to want all the credit for the job, blinded him in a great degree to the truth. Hence we find him protecting his own sons from the blessings that had been his. Instead of having his boys brought up to do things, he had servants who cheated them out of all that round of daily duties which had made him strong. He had tutors who taught them things out of books and gave them advice. The result was that the sons of George M. Pullman have achieved guardians and their fantastic tricks before high heaven have added to the gayety of nations 🙞

Pullman's boys are without even a trace of that decision and strength that made their father famous. George M. Pullman could operate a great industry, but he

129

could not bring up a family. He succeeded
in everything but the boy business.

Of course, we cannot assume that these
boys would have been as competent as
their father had they been brought up to
work, but work would have, at least, protected them from excess.

The method pursued by George M. Pullman in educating his boys is the plan pursued by most rich men. All that they gain
for the world is lost again in their
children ✒

And until yesterday all the college presi-
dents and all the pedagogs who lectured
and taught and wrote and preached, fully
endorsed the plan adopted by George M.
Pullman in educating his boys.

So sternly true is this that Dr. Edward
Everett Hale, a graduate of Harvard, has
said, "If you should take twelve prize
men from Harvard and put them on a
sinking ship, they would all drown through
inability to construct a raft."

The mole-blind pedagogs are quite willing
to keep on stuffing boys with impressions,
not knowing that the number of impressions a boy can hold is limited. We grow
through expression, and the large colleges,

130

even yet, afford a very imperfect means for expression—all is impression and repression and suppression.

But to-day we find a few of the highest type of teachers making a bold stand for the natural method of education. That is, they recognize that the education which George M. Pullman received was a better, wiser and safer education than the education which George M. Pullman gave to his boys ☞

Recently I visited the John Dewey School at Chicago, and there I saw them doing for the children, with carefully prepared intent, just what fate, poverty & " unkind conditions " did for George M. Pullman. ☞ John Dewey, the head of the Dewey School, is a pupil of that noted psychologist and thoroughly sane man, Dr. Stanley Hall ; and the cry of Dr. Hall is " Back to Nature."

At the Dewey School they try to teach children just as a kind, intelligent and loving mother would teach her children if she lived away off forty miles from nowhere, and had an income of three hundred dollars a year to support a family of nine ☞

131

Nothing interests us save as it comes home to us as a personal issue. And in visiting the Dewey School I unconsciously compared it with my own early lack of instruction ✍

When I was fifteen years of age I could break wild horses to saddle or harness, and teach kicking cows to stand while they were being milked. I could fell trees and drop the tree in any direction desired; I knew the relative value of all native woods; appreciated the difference in soil, grains, fruits and simple minerals. I could use the drawshave, adz, axe, broad-axe, crosscut saw, sickle and cradle. I could make a figure-four trap, an axe helve, a neckyoke, ox yoke, whiffletrees, clevis, and braid an eight-strand cattle whip. We used to mend our harness on rainy days, and I could make a wax end and thread it with a bristle and use a brad awl. I knew how to construct an ash leach and to make soft soap, apple butter and pump-kin pies. I knew the process of weaving flax and wool, of making and burning brick. I knew on sight and had names for a score or more of birds, and had a good idea of the habits of squirrels, skunks,

132

wolves and the fishes that swam in the
creeks. I knew how to cure hams, shoul-
ders & sidemeat ; to pickle beef, and cover
apples with straw and earth so they would
keep in safety through the most severe
winter, and open up in the spring fresh
and valuable ✒

Of course, my knowledge was not of the
scientific order, and I could not have explained it to another, because I never knew
I had it. It all came along easily, naturally and as a matter of course. It would
be absurd to say that I was an expert
worker in all the lines I have mentioned,
but I was familiar with the processes and
could do things with my hands all in my
own crude way, just as I daily saw my
father and the neighbors doing.

And so when I saw at this experimental
school of Chicago University the same
curriculum that I had known in youth
being worked out I could not but smile.
Professor John Dewey, with his costly
apparatus and heavy endowment, is merely trying to overcome the " advantages "
of civilization ✒

They have no wild horses nor kicking
cows in the Dewey School, but they teach

children to make things out of wood, iron and cloth. They are taught to measure, weigh, compare and decide. They wash dishes and put things away in a neat and orderly manner. They are taught the nature of wool, cotton and flax, and are shown how to weave, dye and construct. They learn without knowing when or how they learn. The repression and discipline that one feels in many schools is removed and there is an air of freedom in the place that is very helpful. It's a curious experiment—this back to nature—but in the line of truth ☞

There is no more preposterous admonition than that which has been dinged into the ears of innocence for centuries, that "Children should be seen and not heard." ☞ The healthy, active child is full of impressions and that he should express himself is just as natural as for a bird to sing. It is nature's way of giving growth—no one knows a thing for sure until he tells it to someone else. We deepen impressions by recounting them, and habitually to suppress and repress the child when he wants to tell of the curious things he has seen, is to fly in the face of God.

Last summer on a horseback ride of a hundred miles or so I came to an out-of- the-way " Deestrick School," just such a one as you see every three miles all over New York State. This particular school house would not have attracted my attention specially had I not noticed that nearly half the school lot was taken up with a garden and flower beds. No house was near, and it was apparent that this garden was the work of the teacher and pupils. ✺ Straightway I dismounted, tied my horse and walked into the school house ✺ The teacher was a man of middle age—a hunchback and one of the rarest, gentlest spirits I ever met. Have you ever noticed what an alert, receptive and beautiful soul is often housed in a misshapen body ? This man was modest and shy as a woman, & when I spoke of the flower beds he half apologized for them and tried to change the subject. When after a few moments he realized that my interest in his garden was something deeper than mere curiosity, he offered to go out and show me what had been done. So we walked out, and out, too, behind us trooped the school of just fifteen children ✺

135

" In winter we have sixty or more pupils, but you see the school is small now. I thought I would try the plan of teaching out of doors half the time, and to keep the girls and boys busy I just let each scholar have a flower bed. Some wanted to raise vegetables and of course I let them plant any seed they wished. The older children, girls or boys, help the younger ones—it is lots of fun. When the weather is fine we are out here a good deal of the time, just working and talking," explained the teacher.

And that is the way this man taught—letting the children do things and talk. He explained to me that he was not an " educated " man, and as I contradicted him my eyes filled with tears. Not educated? I wonder how many of us who call ourselves educated have a disciplined mind, and can call by name the forest birds in our own vicinity? Do we know the bird notes when we hear them? Can we with pencil outline the leaves of oak, elm, walnut, maple, chestnut, hazel, birch or beech trees, so that others, familiar with these trees, can recognize them?

Do we know by name or on sight the

insects that fill the summer night with melody? Do we know whether the katy-did, cricket and locust "sing" with mouth, wings or feet? Do we know what they feed upon, how long they live, and what becomes of the tree-toad in winter?

I wonder what it is to be educated! Here was a man seemingly sore smitten by the hand of Fate, and yet whose heart was filled with sympathy and love. He had no quarrel with either the world or Destiny. He was childless that he might love all children, and that his heart might go out to every living thing. The trustees of the school did not take much interest in the curriculum, I found, so they let the teacher have his way. A collection of birds' eggs, fungi and forest leaves had been made, and I was shown outline drawings of all the leaves in the garden. This idea of drawing a picture of the object led to a closer observation, the teacher thought. And when I found on questioning some of the children, that the whole school took semi-weekly rambles through the woods, and made close studies of the wild birds, as well as insects, it came to me that this man, far from any "intellectual center,"

137

A MESSAGE was working out a pedagogic system that TO GARCIA science could never improve upon. Now whether the little man realized this or not I cannot say, but I do not think he guessed the greatness of his work and methods. It was all so simple—he did the thing he liked to do, and led the children out, and they followed because they loved the man and soon loved the things that he loved. ❧ Science seeks to simplify. This country school teacher, doing his own little work in his own little way, was a true scientist. And in the presence of such a man should we not uncover?

The success of an individual is usually damnation for his children. Luxury enervates and kills, and this is the reason that the race has made such slow and painful progress. All one generation gains is lost in the next. The great nations have died off from the earth simply because they succeeded. The grandeur that was Greece and the glory that was Rome are but names writ in water. The splendours of Spain and Italy are crumbling into dust. Whether France and England have not expressed their best is a question—nations like families die the death and they die

138

because they win ✎ Institutions similar to the Dewey School are attempts to hold the ground once gained, and as such they should command the earnest considera- tion and respect of every man who knows history and who realizes that the progress of civilization has been only a repetition of the labor of Sisyphus.

We grow strong through doing things And when one generation comes into pos- session of the material good that the for- mer generation has gained, and makes that fool remark, " I do n't have to work," it straightway is stepping on the chute that gives it a slide to Avernus—and then all has to be done over again.

I expect to see the day when school teachers will not be supplied a beautiful scarcity of everything but hard work.

I expect to see the day when no school teacher will have more than twenty pupils. ✎ I expect to see the day when the hon- ors and compensation of school teaching will command the services of the best and strongest men and women in every community ✎

I expect to see the day when the conver- sational method will be supreme, and teaching will be done practically without books—by object lessons, thinking things out and doing things.

I expect to see the day when overwrought nerves in teacher or pupil will be unknown, for joy will take the place of anxiety, and all the bugaboo of "exams" will be consigned to limbo. The evolution even now is at work, and the time is ripe. The beauty seen in all school rooms, and the reaching out for harmony are not in vain. These things are bearing fruit.

This is the richest country the world has ever known. We are loaning money to Europe—and ideas, too. We spend a sum total in America of two hundred million dollars a year for the support of our public schools. Yet we raised a like sum last year for war and fighting machines, and no one lifted an eyebrow, except a few cranks around Boston and a man in Nebraska

Now suppose that we awaken to the truth that war is waste, and worse,—that we stand in no danger and need few soldiers, and that we would better educate our boys and girls at home than indulge in doubtful Old World experiments—then

what! Why, we 'll reduce our fighting
force and use the money to increase the
efficiency of our teaching force. We will
let children grow strong and unfold
through doing things and talking about
them as they do them, and pupils and
teacher will grow strong together. We will
do away with truancy, trampism, hoodlumism and lessen crime by nine-tenths.
We will not suppress bad or restless boys,
we will divert them and direct their energies into paths of usefulness. And the day
is coming ✍

For these thoughts are not my thoughts.
They are in the hearts of thousands in
every city, town, hamlet and village—east
or west, north or south—it 's just God's
truth ✍

And when enough people arrive at
Truth, and realize that every day is Judg-
ment Day, and the important place is
Here, and the time is Now, then we will
work for a present good, and educate, not
kill; love, not hate; and the men and
women who educate most and best shall
be honored most. The Day is dawning in
the East ✍

141

THE BETTER
PART

I AM an Anarchist A MESSAGE TO GARCIA All good men are Anarchists.

All cultured and kindly men; all gentle men; all just men are Anarchists. ❧ Jesus was an Anarchist.

A Monarchist is one who believes a monarch should govern. A Plutocrat believes in the rule of the rich. A Democrat holds that the majority should dictate. An Aristocrat thinks only the wise should decide; while an Anarchist does not believe in government at all.

Richard Croker is a Monarchist; Mark Hanna is a Plutocrat; Cleveland a Democrat; Cabot Lodge an Aristocrat; William Penn, Henry D. Thoreau, Bronson Alcott and Walt Whitman were Anarchists.

An Anarchist is one who minds his own business. An Anarchist does not believe in sending war ships across wide oceans to kill brown men, and lay waste rice fields, and burn the homes of people who are fighting for liberty. An Anarchist does not drive women with babes at the breast and other women with babes unborn, children and old men into the jungle to be devoured by beasts or fever or fear, or die of hunger, homeless, unhouseled and undone ℱ

Destruction, violence, ravages and murder are perpetrated by statute law. Without law there would be no infernal machines, no war ships, no dynamite guns, no flat-nosed bullets, no pointed cartridges, no bayonets, no policemen's billies, no night sticks, no come-alongs, no handcuffs, no straight jackets, no dark cells, no gallows, no prison walls to conceal the infamies therein inflicted. Without law no little souls fresh from God would be branded "illegitimate" indelibly as soon as they reach Earth. Without law there would be less liars, no lawyers, fewer hypocrites and no Devil's Island.

The Cry of the Little Peoples goes up to God
    in vain,
For the world is given over to the cruel sons of
    Cain ;
The hand that would bless us is weak, and the
    hand that would break us is strong,
And the power of pity is naught but the power
    of a song.
The dreams that our fathers dreamed to-day are
    laughter and dust,

148

And nothing at all in the world is left for a man
    to trust.
Let us hope no more, nor dream, nor prophesy,
    nor pray,
For the iron world no less will crash on its iron
    way;
And nothing is left but to watch, with a helpless
    pitying eye,
The kind old aims for the world, and the kind
    old fashions die.

I do not go quite so far as that—I'm a pessimistic-optimist, Dearie, — I believe that brutality tends to defeat itself. Prize fighters die young, gourmands get the gout, hate hurts worse the man who nurses it, and all selfishness robs the mind of its divine insight and cheats the soul that would know. Mind alone is eternal! He, watching over Israel, slumbers not nor sleeps. My faith is great: out of the transient darkness of the present the shadows will flee away, and Day will yet dawn.
I am an Anarchist.
No man who believes in force and violence is an Anarchist. The true Anarchist decries all influences save those of love and reason. Ideas are his only arms.
Being an Anarchist I am also a Socialist. Socialism is the antithesis of Anarchy.

149

One is the North Pole of Truth, the other the South. The Socialist believes in working for the good of all, while Anarchy is pure Individualism. I believe in every man working for the good of self; and in working for the good of self, he works for the good of all. To think, to see, to feel, to know; to deal justly; to bear all patiently; to act quietly; to speak cheerfully; to moderate one's voice—these things will bring you the highest good. They will bring you the love of the best and the esteem of that Sacred Few whose good opinion alone is worth cultivating. And further than this, it is the best way you can serve Society—live your life. The wise way to benefit humanity is to attend to your own affairs, and thus give other people an opportunity to look after theirs.

If there is any better way to teach virtue than by practicing it, I do not know it.

Would you make men better—set them an example ✍

The Millennium will never come until governments cease from governing, and the meddler is at rest. Politicians are men who volunteer the task of governing us for a consideration. The political boss is intent on living off your labor. A man may seek an office in order to do away with the rascal who now occupies it, but for the most part office-seekers are rank rogues. Shakespeare uses the word politician five times, and each time it is synonymous with knave. That is to say, a politician is one who sacrifices truth and honor for policy. The highest motive of his life is expediency—policy. In King Lear it is the "scurvy politician," who through tattered clothes beholds small vices, while robes and furred gowns, for him, cover all.

Europe is divided up between eight great governments, and in time of peace over three million men are taken from the ranks of industry and are under arms, not to protect the people, but to protect one government from another.

Mankind is governed by the worst—the strongest example of this is to be seen in American municipalities, but it is true of every government ⚡

We are governed by rogues who hold their grip upon us by and through statute law. Were it not for law the people could protect themselves against these thieves, but now we are powerless and are robbed legally ✿ One mild form of coercion these rogues resort to, is to call us unpatriotic when we speak the truth about them. Not long ago they would have cut off our heads. The world moves.

Governments cannot be done away with instantaneously, but progress will come, as it has in the past, by lessening the number of laws. We want less governing, and the Ideal Government will arrive when there is no government at all.

So long as governments set the example of killing their enemies, private individuals will occasionally kill theirs.

So long as men are clubbed, robbed, imprisoned, disgraced, hanged by the governing class, just so long will the idea of violence and brutality be born in the souls of men ✿

Governments imprison men, and then hound them when they are released.

Hate springs eternal in the human breast. ✿ And hate will never die so long as men are taken from useful production on the specious plea of patriotism, and bayonets gleam in God's pure sunshine.

And the worst part about making a soldier of a man is, not that the soldier kills brown men or black men or white men, but it is that the soldier loses his own soul ✒

I am an Anarchist.

I do not believe in bolts or bars or brutality. I make my appeal to the Divinity in men, and they, in some mysterious way, feeling this, do not fail me.

I send valuable books, without question, on a postal card request, to every part of the Earth where the mail can carry them, and my confidence is never abused. The Roycroft Shop is never locked, employees and visitors come and go at pleasure, and nothing is molested. My library is for anyone who cares to use it.

Out in the great world women occasionally walk off the dock in the darkness, and then struggle for life in the deep waters. Society jigs and ambles by, with a coil of rope, but before throwing it demands of the sinking one a certificate of character from her Pastor or a letter of recommendation from her Sunday School Superintendent, or a testimonial from a School Principal. Not being able to produce the document, the struggler is left to go down to her death in the darkness.

A so-called " bad woman " is usually one
whose soul is being rent in an awful tra-
vail of prayer to God that she may get
back upon solid footing and lead an honest
life. Believing this, the Roycroft principle
is never to ask for such a preposterous
thing as a letter of recommendation from
anyone. We have two hundred helpers,
and while it must not be imagined by any
means that we operate a reform school
or a charitable institution, I wish to say
that I distinctly and positively refuse to
discriminate between " good " and " bad "
people. I will not condemn, nor for an in-
stant imagine that it is my duty to resolve
myself into a section of the Day of Judg-
ment ✍

I fix my thought on the good that is in
every soul and make my appeal to that.
And the plan is a wise one, judged by re-
sults. It secures you loyal helpers, worthy
friends, gets the work done, aids digestion
and tends to sleep o' nights. And I say to
you, that if you have never known the
love, loyalty and integrity of a proscribed
person, you have never known what love,
loyalty and integrity are ✍ I do not believe in governing by force, or threat, or

154

any other form of coercion. I would not arouse in the heart of any of God's creatures a thought of fear, or discord, or hate, or revenge. I will influence men, if I can, but it shall be only by aiding them to think for themselves; and so mayhap, they, of their own accord, will choose the better part—the ways that lead to life and light.

THE CRYING
NEED

THE Servant Girl is a property used by all humorists in Class B; and the troubles of the Mistress are a recurring theme in every club and editorial room.

The wailings of the Woman who has employed a Cook-lady form a subdued anvil chorus that hums the round world over as the earth revolves, like the drum-taps of Great Britain on which the sun never sets—but may.

The Woes of the Mistress! They will never down—and as a topic for conversation the Servant Girl question will remain with us just as long as does the Servant Girl. I think, however, although I may be all wrong, that it is the Mistress that needs reformation—not the Girl.

The Servant Girl system draws a sharp line of demarcation between the Girl and the Mistress. The Mistress fights to keep the line more deeply etched—the Girl strives to obliterate it.

And the Girl will win—and some day I 'll tell you why.

But there is a Chorus of Kickers that

A MESSAGE growls its thunderous bass in a manner
TO GARCIA just as pronounced as the shrill falsetto of
the Amalgamated Mistresses. And yet no
funny man has ever made note of the bass,
while the soprano is worked over-time ❦
The Kick to which I refer is the wail of
every man who operates a store, shop,
factory, bank, railroad or any other institution that employs many men.
Every Successful Concern is the result of
a One-Man Power. Co-operation, tech-
nically, is an iridescent dream — things
co-operate because the Man makes them.
He cements them by his will.
But find this Man, and get his confidence
and his weary eyes will look into yours
and the cry of his heart shall echo in your
ears, "O for someone to help me bear this
burden!"
Then he will tell you of his endless search
for Ability, and of his continual disap-
pointments and thwartings in trying to
get someone to help himself by helping
him ❦
Ability is the one crying need of the hour.
❦ The banks are bulging with money,
everywhere are men wanting work. The
harvest is ripe.

162

But the Ability to captain the unemployed and utilize the capital is lacking—sadly lacking ✒

In every city there are dozens of five and ten thousand dollar a year positions to be filled, but the only applicants are men who want a job at fifteen dollars a week. Your man of Ability has a place already.

Yes, Ability is a rare article.

But there is something that is much more scarce, something finer far, something rarer than Ability.

It is the Ability to recognize Ability.

The sternest comment that can be made against employers as a class lies in the fact that men of Ability usually succeed in showing their worth in spite of their employer, and not with his assistance and encouragement ✒

If you know the lives of men of Ability, you know that they discovered their power, almost without exception, through accident. Had the accident not occurred that made the opportunity, the man would have been practically lost to the world ✒

The experience of Tom Potter, the telegraph operator, at an obscure little way station, is truth painted large. That fearful

163

night, when most of the wires were down
and a passenger train went through the
bridge, gave Tom Potter the opportunity
of discovering himself. He took charge of
the dead, cared for the wounded, settled
fifty claims—drawing drafts on the company—burned the last vestige of the
wreck, sunk the waste iron in the river
and repaired the bridge before the Superintendent arrived on the spot.

" Who gave you authority to do all this ? "
demanded the Superintendent.

"Nobody," said Tom, "I assumed the
authority."

The next month Tom Potter's salary was
$5,000 a year, and in three years he was
making ten times this, simply because he
could get other men to do things.

Why wait for an accident to discover
Tom Potter? Let us set traps for Tom
Potter, and lie in wait for him. Perhaps
Tom Potter is just around the corner,
across the street, in the next room, or at
our elbow!

I know a man who roamed the woods and
fields for thirty years and never found an
Indian arrow. One day he began to think
" arrow," and stepping out of his doorway

164

he picked one up. Since then he has collected a bushel.

Suppose we cease wailing about incompetence, sleepy indifference and slip-shod "help" that watches the clock. These things exist—let us dispose of the subject by admitting it, and then emphasize the fact that freckled farmer boys come out of the West and East and often go to the front and do things in a masterly way ⚓

There is one name that stands out in history like a beacon light after all these twenty-five hundred years have passed, just because the man had the sublime Genius of discovering Ability.

That man is Pericles.

Pericles made Athens.

And to-day the very dust of the streets of Athens is being sifted and searched for relics and remnants of the things made by people who were captained by men of Ability who were discovered by Pericles. ⚓ There is little competition in this line of discovering Ability. We sit down and wail because Ability does not come our way ⚓

Let us think "Ability" and possibly we can jostle Pericles there on his pedestal, where he has stood for over a score of centuries—the man with a supreme Genius for recognizing Ability ✒ Hail to thee, Pericles, and hail to thee, Great Unknown, who shall first successfully imitate him !

SO HERE ENDETH THE GOODLY BOOK
ENTITLED "A MESSAGE TO GARCIA AND
THIRTEEN OTHER THINGS," AS WRIT-
TEN BY FRA ELBERTUS, AND DONE INTO
PRINT BY THE ROYCROFTERS AT THEIR
SHOP, WHICH IS IN EAST AURORA ❦ ❦

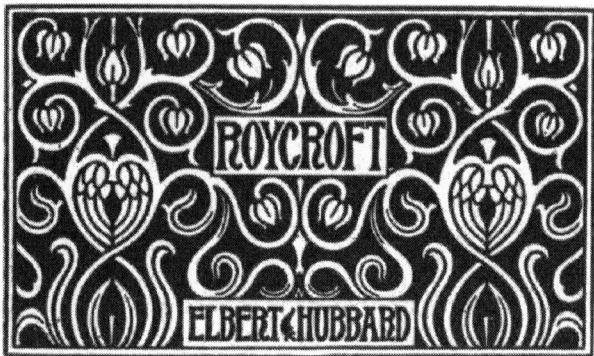
ROYCROFT

ELBERT HUBBARD

CPSIA information can be obtained
at www.ICGtesting.com
Printed in the USA
LVHW010307270423
745458LV00022B/315

9 781016 694759